My Life: A Father's Memories of Life and Learning

My Life: A Father's Memories of Life and Learning

A Journal To Communicate Your Memories, Values and Lessons of Life To Your Child

Susan Kitchen

Writers Club Press
San Jose New York Lincoln Shanghai

My Life: A Father's Memories of Life and Learning
A Journal To Communicate Your Memories, Values and Lessons of Life To Your Child

All Rights Reserved © 2001 by Susan Kitchen

No part of this book may be reproduced or transmitted in any form or by any means, graphic, electronic, or mechanical, including photocopying, recording, taping, or by any information storage retrieval system, without the permission in writing from the publisher.

Writers Club Press
an imprint of iUniverse.com, Inc.

For information address:
iUniverse.com, Inc.
5220 S 16th, Ste. 200
Lincoln, NE 68512
www.iuniverse.com

ISBN: 0-595-18717-X

Printed in the United States of America

Foreword

A father is of the utmost importance to his child. We all assume that fathers know this, but they may not. Recently, my own father has been telling me family history from his side of the family. He has been telling me the stories of his youth that he carries with him even to this day. There are many things that occurred in the world and that happened to my father that are fascinating. My father is now in his seventies and I am in my thirties. As I now listen to him, I think about how wonderful it would have been to have a book like this at various points in my past to draw parallels and to see if we share some of the same human experiences. I am now coming to realize at this late date that my father is a person in his own right, even though I have been fortunate enough to have parents that stayed married and my father always lived with us.

Write in this journal with that in mind. Men do not convey information to their children in the same way that women and mothers do. But know this…your children want to know the real you while you still remain a father and maintain the important influence that comes with this job.

At several points in the life of your children, you may feel as though your influence does not count and is not important. You may feel as though your children do not listen and are not interested in your observations and experiences. Several journals have been written for all kinds of mothers, from those expecting, to those who are now facing their children's impending adulthood. This daughter wants fathers to know that we are interested in your observations and guidance as well. You have not been forgotten, nor will you be if you give us this gift of yourself.

So please, tell us all about you. Be the influence and guide, the storyteller that your child so needs. I know you can. We want to know all about you. Children love their Daddies. Thank you so much for sharing of yourself with us.

My Past

Tell your child about your birth. Where were you born? How much did you weigh? Were you a healthy baby? What was going on in the world the year you were born? Who was President? The number one song? Number one movie? Fashion? List any historical events of note.

Tell your child about your parents. What did they look like? What did they do for a living? Did they have hobbies? Did you see them as people in their own right? How did they show you love? Were they involved in their own culture? Did they convey your cultural identity to you in some significant way?

Tell your child what you remember about your own grandparents. What nationality were they? Where did they finally settle to raise their families? Did they pass on any traditions to you? What did they do for a living? How did they show you love? What did they do with you at family gatherings? What did you love most about them?

What do you remember about your preschool years? Who were your friends? What was your favorite toy? What were you afraid of? What is your first clear memory? Describe what you liked to do to play. What were your favorite games?

Where did you live as a child? Was it the city, suburbs, or was it rural? Did you have neighbors? What do you remember about them? Did you have a favorite hiding place at home? What was your room like? What was your favorite thing about your house? What was your least favorite? Did anything scare you about your house? What kind of yard did you have? Did you like to play outside? Tell your child about your favorite activities outdoors.

Do you have brother and/or sisters? What did you do together? What did you quarrel about? Who did you get along with best? Who is most like you? Who is most different? Were there family traditions centered around the children? What were they? What were your chores and responsibilities? How were they divided? Tell your child your favorite thing about having the brothers and/or sisters that you have.

Tell your child about your first day of school. Where did you go to school? Who was your kindergarten teacher? Did you have a best friend? Who was it? What was your favorite activity at school that year? What did you not like about school, if anything?

Who was the best elementary teacher you had? What is the most significant thing this teacher taught you? What year did you have this teacher? What kind of impact did he /she have on your life? Why did you like him/her so much?

Were you ever bullied in school? Tell your child how this made you feel. What happened? How was the problem finally solved? If you could confront your bully today, as an adult, what would you say? Looking back, from an adult perspective, why do you think this happened? What do you think caused your bully to behave so badly?

Did you ever have a crush as an elementary student? Who was it? How did this person make you feel? Why did you become infatuated with her? What did you do, if anything, to express your feelings for her?

Were you ever seriously hurt as a child, or very ill? Did you have to go to the hospital? Were you scared? How were you comforted? How did it happen? What did you do while you recovered? Did you have the same illness or injury more than once?

Who was your best friend as an elementary age child? What did you do for fun? What absolutely cracked you up? What did you have in common? What was different about this person? What did you talk about? What did you dream about together?

Did you vacation as a young child? Where did you go? Did you take a trip for any other purpose? Tell your child about some of the things you saw or experienced on this trip.

Did you ever have the experience of seeing history unfold on television or hear it on the radio? (Example: the day that Reagan or Kennedy was shot) What were you doing? What had happened? Tell your child about the impact it had on your life and the lives of those around you.

Tell your child what you did to amuse yourself when you were young. What was your favorite toy? What were your favorite games? What did you like to do while alone?

Did you enjoy music when you were young? What bands and songs meant the most to you? Why? What was really popular? Did you like this or was your taste different? Did you go to any concerts? Did you collect albums or posters in a devotion to those you liked?

Did you enjoy television as a child? What were your favorite shows? Did you look forward to the times that they were on? What did you love so much about these shows? Did you have a favorite television actor or character? Who and why?

What was your all-time favorite movie as a child? Favorite character? What was the movie about? Why did this please you? Did it move you in any specific way?

What is the best book you read as a child? What did it teach you? What brought you joy about this story? Did you have to read it for school;, or did you just happen upon it? Tell your child about the impact things you read had upon your life.

Did you have a pet as a child? What kind of pet was it? Tell your child what you loved about this pet. If you had more than one pet, which was your favorite? What did you learn from this pet?

What did you want to do for a living when you grew up? Why did you want to do this? Did you think it be fun, adventurous, or lucrative? Tell your child how you happened to become what you are today in the working world.

Who was your hero as a child? What did you admire most about this person? Was it a real person or a fictional character? Tell your child the qualities which you tried to emulate that this hero possessed.

Do you remember the first time you saw the ocean or a mountain or your first visit to an area that was entirely new to you? (Example: seeing the big city if you grew up in the country) Describe your sense of wonder for your child. Tell your child all that you remember. (Sights, colors, smell, size)

Did your parents ever tell you a myth or falsehood in answer to a question? (Example: "The stork brings babies") If so, what was it? How did you feel when you found out the truth? Why do you think they did this? If they never told you such a story, describe for your child how it was to have been dealt with honestly.

Did you ever want something that you could not have? What was it? What did you do to try and get it? Tell your child the lesson in not getting all that you want.

Describe for your child a rite of passage, like learning to drive. When did this rite take place? How did you know that you had crossed over into young adulthood? Did somebody tell you, or was it just assumed? Tell you child how you felt after crossing the threshold.

Pick one lesson your own parents taught you. Why was this one the most important? Make it words to live by, and pass them on to your child.

What was your first paying job? How did you get it? Tell your child what you thought of money's place in your life before you worked, and how you now view the place of money in your life.

What was the singlemost enjoyable thing that you shared with your own parents? Tell your child what you hope to enjoy with them.

THE PRESENT

Describe yourself today for your child. Tell your child who you are, how tall what you weigh, how you perceive your own appearance, and where you live. How do you think the world sees you?

Tell your child about the day you met his or her mother. How and when did you know that you loved her? What struck you first about this woman? Tell your child about her best qualities. Describe why your love endures, even now.

Describe your spiritual beliefs and practices. Include rituals, holidays, moral beliefs, and how you feel about any afterlife.

What is your greatest skill or talent? How did you find out you had this skill or talent? Describe for your child why this is such an asset, or why it is just fun or unusual.

Describe your political beliefs for your child. Why do you feel as you do about politics and the government? Tell your child about the defining moment when you made the choice to believe as you do.

Tell your child which activities you presently pursue for leisure or a hobby. Describe why you find these activities enjoyable or relaxing.

Describe an instance where you gave something your best effort and still did not succeed. Describe how you dealt with disappointment and managed to overcome it. Give your child advice on how to deal with and overcome disappointment in his or her own life. Tell your child what you learned and now carry with you from this experience.

If you had to live the same day over and over for eternity, what would you do in that twenty-four hours? Describe this perfect day in detail for your child.

If you could remove one event or day from your life, what would it be? How would removing this change you, for better or worse? Even if you could change something, would you?

Tell your child which qualities you look for in a friend as an adult. Do you need to have much in common, or do you enjoy diversity? Are your friends more about talking, or being active? Who is your best friend and why?

What is the most important thing you learned as a teen or young adult? Describe the situation or circumstances when you learned this. Why was it so important to your life to have this knowledge?

Who do you feel the most influential people from history have been? Why? What kind of influence did they have on the world and on your life?

If you won the lottery or in some way became suddenly wealthy, tell your child what you would do with the money. Would you be supportive of charity, buy the house you've dreamed of, quit work? Give details of what you'd purchase with newfound wealth and why.

Tell your child about a place you've never been that you'd really like to visit. Where is it? What do you hope to see there? How long have you wanted to go?

What is your best quality? Tell your child why you think this is your best quality. Describe what you do in your life to ensure that you best use this gift.

What is your worst quality? Can you change this? Do you want to change this? Tell your child why you think this is your worst quality.

If you had to pick ten items and live on a deserted island, tell your child what they'd be and why you'd choose these ten.

Who is the most courageous person you've ever known? What constitutes courage? Tell your child about this person and the actions they took to demonstrate courage.

Tell your child what justice means to you. Explain some instances of justice and injustice that you've seen in your lifetime.

Tell your child about a piece of work that you find productive and rewarding. (Example: gardening or woodworking) Tell your child the benefits you've reaped from hard work.

Tell your child about a piece of work or a duty that you dread doing. Explain why you do it anyway.

Tell your child what makes someone a good man. List the qualities and attributes that a good man should have. Tell your child about some good men you've known. Tell your child what makes someone a good father. List the qualities that you hope to attain as a father.

Make a list of the people you love and why you love them.

BECOMING A FATHER

Tell your child how you found out that his or her mother was expecting. Were you surprised? Explain any insight you gained during the pregnancy. Address any issue that really had a profound impact on your way of thinking.

Tell your child what your thoughts were as you witnessed his or her birth or first had the opportunity to see them.

Tell your child about the things that you found to be unique as you went through infancy with them. Explain the things that nobody had prepared you for and the things that you found funny, touching, and very unexpected.

Tell your child about an inequality of the human condition that you'd like to see corrected in his or her lifetime. Do have any ideas of how to rectify this situation?

Tell your child about things you swore to never try and do as a a parent. Is there any of these things that you'd now like to change your thinking on? Why?

What did you most respect about your own parents? What are the qualities that they had that you'd like to have? How can you achieve this?

LETTERS TO YOUR CHILD

Each year on your child's birthday, write them a letter on these pages. Be sure to include any changes in yourself. Tell your child about events in your life over the past year. Tell your child about the changes you've observed in them, how they've grown, what they've achieved, and things you've observed them learning.

Your first birthday:

Your second birthday:

Your third birthday:

Your fourth birthday:

Your fifth birthday:

Your sixth birthday:

Your seventh birthday:

Your eighth birthday:

Your ninth birthday:

Your tenth birthday:

Your eleventh birthday:

Your twelfth birthday:

Your thirteenth birthday:

Your fourteenth birthday:

Your fifteenth birthday:

Your sixteenth birthday:

Your seventeenth birthday:

Your eighteenth birthday:

Your nineteenth birthday:

Your twentieth birthday:

Your twenty-first birthday:

CPSIA information can be obtained at www.ICGtesting.com
Printed in the USA
238655LV00003B/190/A